D0339035

PROPERTY OF:
RANCHO MIRAGE PUBLIC LIBRARY
71100 HIGHWAY 111
RANCHO MIRAGE, CA 92270
(760)341-READ (7323)

BRUSSELS STYLE

BRUSSELS

Exteriors Interiors

STYLE

Details

EDITOR **Angelika Taschen**

TASCHEN

Front cover: Rhapsody in blue: Agnes Emery's kitchen.
Couverture : Heure bleue : dans la cuisine d'Agnès Emery.
Umschlagvorderseite: Blaue Stunde: In der Küche von Agnes Emery.
Photo: Alexander van Berge / Taverne Agency

Back cover: A house in harmony with nature: dining area in the style of van Duysen.
Dos de Couverture : Maison en harmonie avec la nature : espace repas dans le style de van Duysen.
Umschlagrückseite: Natur und Haus in Harmonie: Essplatz im Stil von van Duysen.
Photo: Jean-Luc Laloux

To stay informed about upcoming TASCHEN titles, please request our magazine
at www.taschen.com/magazine or write to TASCHEN, Hohenzollernring 53, D-50672 Cologne,
Germany, contact@taschen.com, fax: +49-221-254919. We will be happy to send you a free copy
of our magazine which is filled with information about all of our books.

© 2006 TASCHEN GmbH
Hohenzollernring 53, D-50672 Köln
www.taschen.com

© 2006 for the works by Victor Horta, VG Bild-Kunst, Bonn

Concept and editing by Angelika Taschen, Berlin
Layout and general project management by Stephanie Bischoff, Cologne
Texts by Christiane Reiter, Hamburg
Lithography by Thomas Grell, Cologne
English translation by Isabel Varea, Grapevine Publishing Services, London
French translation by Anne Charrière, Croissy/Seine

Printed in China
ISBN 978-3-8228-2384-2

CONTENTS SOMMAIRE INHALT

Brussels is the capital of Europe with its international politics and its international arts scene. Here, influences from different countries and diverse cultures have always played an important role. For centuries Brussels, a city built on commerce, has readily turned to architecture to parade its prosperity – as can be seen from the old black and white photographs in the first chapter of this book. For example, the Hôtel de Ville, or City Hall, is the perfect embodiment of Brabant Gothic. Its sumptuously-decorated façade seems to swim before the eyes. All around the Grand Place, the guild houses compete for attention with their turrets and gables, balconies and balustrades, statues and reliefs, all providing an enchanting Baroque backdrop to life in the square. The most perfect and sophisticated manifestation of Brussels's architectural style is provided by the Art Nouveau buildings dating from the end of the nineteenth century. Victor Horta, who built the Hôtel Tassel in 1893, and Paul Hankar, who designed his own house in the same year,

CAPITAL OF CULTURE
Christiane Reiter

Bruxelles est la capitale de l'Europe avec son rôle politique international et son rayonnement culturel. Depuis toujours les influences de cultures et de pays différents se croisent ici. Il y a des siècles déjà, la ville marchande de Bruxelles manifestait volontiers son aisance à travers la richesse de son architecture. C'est ce dont témoignent les anciennes photos en noir et blanc au début de ce livre. L'hôtel de ville, par exemple, incarne le gothique brabant par excellence – sa façade est si luxuriante que c'en est presque un éblouissement. Un décors baroque de rêve entoure la Grand'Place, avec ses maisons des corporations qui rivalisent entre elles de tourelles, pignons, balcons, balustrades, figures et reliefs. Reflets de cette architecture bruxelloise raffinée jusqu'à la perfection, les maisons Art Nouveau virent le jour à la fin du XIXᵉ siècle. Victor Horta, qui construisit en 1893 l'« Hôtel Tassel » et Paul Hankar, qui dessina la même année sa propre maison, furent les premiers architectes à miser sur les structures métalliques, les pièces inondées de lumière et des

Brüssel ist die Hauptstadt Europas – mit einer internationalen Politikszene und einer internationalen Kunstszene. Seit jeher spielen hier Einflüsse aus verschiedenen Ländern und Kulturen eine Hauptrolle. Schon vor Jahrhunderten zeigte die Handelsstadt Brüssel ihren Reichtum gerne mit Hilfe der Architektur – das beweisen die historischen Schwarz-Weiß-Aufnahmen im ersten Kapitel dieses Buches. Das Rathaus beispielsweise verkörpert die Brabanter Gotik par excellence – seine Fassade ist so opulent gestaltet, dass es einem fast vor den Augen flimmert. Eine barocke Traumkulisse umgibt die Grand'Place mit ihren Zunfthäusern, die sich gegenseitig mit Türmchen und Giebelchen, Balkonen und Balustraden, Figuren und Reliefs Konkurrenz machen. Und Spiegelbilder der bis zur Perfektion verfeinerten Brüsseler Baukunst sind die Jugendstil-Häuser – die Art-Nouveau-Gebäude, die Ende des 19. Jahrhunderts entstanden. Victor Horta, der 1893 das »Hôtel Tassel« baute, und Paul Hankar, der im selben Jahr sein eigenes Wohnhaus entwarf,

were the first architects to take advantage of metal construction, create spaces flooded with light, and use motifs like arabesques, plants or feminine silhouettes to fashion a whole new living environment. Even now, in an Art Nouveau building, its feels as though one has entered a complete, three-dimensional work of art. From wrought-iron grilles by way of glass vases to mosaics, everything is perfectly coordinated and interwoven to form a coherent whole. Even posters, gold jewellery and ceramics seem as though they were designed exclusively for this house, this wall or that shelf. The flowing lines and geometric shapes – reminders of the Vienna Secession – are found throughout the houses built by Horta, Hankar and other great architects like Ernest Blérot and Henry van de Velde. They create an ambiance of creativity, elegance and harmony which can also be seen in the flats and houses in Chapters two and three, furnished by art connoisseurs such as Axel Vervoordt, Lionel Jadot and Eugénie Collet.

motifs tels que arabesques, plantes et silhouettes féminines pour créer de tout nouveaux environnements de vie. Aujourd'hui encore, on se sent dans une maison Art Nouveau comme à l'intérieur d'une œuvre totale en trois dimensions. De la grille en fer forgé au vase de verre, en passant par la mosaïque, tout s'engrène comme les dents d'un pignon de roue. Même les affiches, la joaillerie et les céramiques semblent avoir été faites spécialement pour telle maison, tel mur ou telle étagère. Les lignes ondulantes et les formes géométriques – souvenirs de la Sécession viennoise – investissent les édifices de Horta, de Hankar et d'autres grands architectes tels que Ernest Blérot ou Henry van de Velde. Elles créent une atmosphère pleine de créativité, d'élégance et d'harmonie, que l'on retrouve également dans les appartements et les maisons montrés dans le deuxième tiers de ce livre. Ceux-ci ont été aménagés par des connaisseurs d'art tel que Axel Vervoordt, Lionel Jadot ou Eugénie Collet.

waren die ersten Architekten, die auf Metallstrukturen, lichtdurchflutete Räume und Motive wie Arabesken, Pflanzen oder weibliche Silhouetten setzten und damit ganze Lebenswelten schufen. Noch heute fühlt man sich in einem Art-Nouveau-Haus wie in einem dreidimensionalen Gesamtkunstwerk. Vom schmiedeeisernen Gitter über die Glasvase bis hin zum Mosaik greift alles wie ein Zahnrad ins andere; selbst Plakate, Goldschmuck und Keramiken wirken so, als seien sie ausschließlich für dieses Haus, diese Wand oder dieses Regal geschaffen worden. Die schwingenden Linien und die geometrischen Formen – Souvenirs der Wiener Sezession – durchziehen die Gebäude von Horta, Hankar und weiteren großen Architekten wie Ernest Blérot oder Henry van de Velde. Sie schaffen ein Ambiente der Kreativität, Eleganz und Harmonie, das auch in den Wohnungen und Häusern zu finden ist, die im zweiten und dritten Kapitel gezeigt werden und von den Kunstkennern wie Axel Vervoordt, Lionel Jadot oder Eugénie Collet ausgestattet wurden.

"... Those were the days when Brussels dreamed
Those were the days of the silent movies
Those were the days when Brussels sang
Those were the days when Brussels was Brussels ..."

Jacques Brel, *from the song "Bruxelles"*

« ... C'était au temps où Bruxelles rêvait
C'était au temps du cinéma muet
C'était au temps où Bruxelles chantait
C'était au temps où Bruxelles bruxellait ... »

Jacques Brel, *extrait de la chanson « Bruxelles »*

» ... Es war die Zeit, in der Brüssel träumte
Es war die Stummfilmzeit
Es war die Zeit, in der Brüssel sang
Es war die Zeit, in der Brüssel brüsselte ... «

Jacques Brel, aus dem Lied *»Bruxelles«*

EXTERIORS

Extérieurs   Aussichten

10/11 Rebuilt according to the original plans: the Maison du Roi in the Grand Place, 1890. *Reconstruite d'après les plans originaux : la « Maison du Roi » sur la Grand'Place, 1890.* Nach Originalplänen rekonstruiert: Die »Maison du Roi« an der Grand'Place, 1890. *Photo: akg-images*

12/13 On his high horse: monument to Godefroy de Bouillon in the Place Royale, c. 1890. *Fière allure : statue équestre de Godefroi de Bouillon sur la Place Royale, vers 1890.* Hoch zu Ross: Das Denkmal Gottfrieds von Bouillon auf der Place Royale, um 1890. *Photo: akg-images*

14/15 Treasures of the sea: Brussels fish market c.1900. *Trésors de la mer : le marché aux poissons de Bruxelles, vers 1900.* Die Schätze des Meeres: Der Brüsseler Fischmarkt, um 1900.
Photo: Hulton Archive / Getty Images

16/17 The heart of the economy: Brussels Stock Exchange built by Leon Suys, 1910. *Au cœur de l'économie : la Bourse construite par Leon Suys, 1910.* Das Herz der Wirtschaft: Die von Leon Suys erbaute Börse, 1910. *Photo: akg-images*

18/19 A meeting point: view of the Brussels Nord Station and two luxury hotels, 1940. *Points de rencontre : vue de la Garde du Nord et deux hôtels de luxe , 1940.* Treffpunkt : Blick auf den Nordbahnhof und zwei Luxushotels, 1940. *Photo: Getty Images*

20/21 Lots of activity: on the Boulevard d'Anspach, c. 1900. *Beaucoup de circulation : sur le Boulevard d'Anspach, vers 1900.* Viel Verkehr: Auf dem Boulevard d'Anspach, um 1900.
Photo: akg-images

22/23 New acquaintances: an amusing assortment at the flea market, 1946. *Étrange rencontre : on trouve de tout sur le marché aux Puces, 1946.* Neue Bekanntschaften: Skurriles Sammelsurium auf dem Flohmarkt, 1946.
Photo: akg-images / Paul Almasy

24/25 Of global significance: the Atomium during the Universal Exhibition 1958. *De portée mondiale : l'Atomium, lors de l'Exposition Universelle de 1958.* Von globaler Bedeutung: Das Atomium während der Weltausstellung 1958. *Photo: akg-images / Paul Almasy*

26/27 An enlarged version of an iron molecule: the Atomium is more than 100m high. *Agrandissement d'une molécule de glace : l'Atomium, plus de 100m de haut.* Die Vergrößerung eines Eisenmoleküls: Das mehr als 100 m hohe Atomium. *Photo: akg-images / Paul Almasy*

28/29 United: the flags of the ten member states of the European Commission, 1981. *Unis : les drapeaux des dix Etats membres de la Communauté européenne, 1981.* Vereint: Die Flaggen der zehn Mitgliedsstaaten des Europäischen Komitees, 1981. *Photo: Getty Images*

30/31 One of the first Art Nouveau buildings: Paul Hankar's house, 1893. *L'un des premiers édifices Art Nouveau : la maison de Paul Hankar, 1893.* Eines der ersten Art-Nouveau-Gebäude: Das Wohnhaus von Paul Hankar, 1893. *Photo: akg-images / Hilbich*

32/33 Everything's in blossom: the Chemiserie Niguet (1896) by Paul Hankar, later became a florist's. *Florissante : la chemiserie Niguet (1896) par Paul Hankar, plus tard un magasin de fleurs.* Alles blüht: Die von Paul Hankar erbaute Chemiserie Niguet (1896), später ein Blumenladen. *Photo: akg-images / Hilbich*

"... Here and there on the walls one could see symbols and ancient emblems in bas-relief: grapes, a glove or a beer mug ...."

Juliusz Kaden, in: *Proch*

« ... Sur les murs, on voyait par endroits les symboles et les emblèmes anciens gravés dans les bas-reliefs : des grappes, un gant ou une chope de bière ... »

Juliusz Kaden, dans: *Proch*

» ... An den Wänden sah man da und dort die in den Flachreliefs eingearbeiteten Symbole und alten Embleme: Trauben, einen Handschuh oder einen Bierkrug ...«

Juliusz Kaden, in: *Proch*

INTERIORS

Intérieurs   Einsichten

38/39 In perfect shape: the dining room at the Musée Horta in Rue Américaine. *Formes parfaites : salle à manger dans le musée Horta, Rue Américaine.* Formvollendet: Speisezimmer im Musée Horta in der Rue Américaine.
Photo: akg-images / Erich Lessing

40/41 Flooded with light: Victor Horta's former residence, since 1969 the Musée Horta. *Baigné de lumière : l'ancienne maison de Victor Horta, depuis 1969 musée Horta.* Lichtdurchflutet: ehemaliges Wohnhaus von Victor Horta, seit 1969 Musée Horta. *Photo: akg-images / Hilbich*

42/43 Surprisingly simple: bedroom at the Musée Horta. *Etonnamment sobre : chambre à coucher au Musée Horta.* Überraschend schlicht: Schlafzimmer im Musée Horta.
Photo: akg-images / Hilbich

44/45 Looking heavenwards: the fanlight in the Maison Hankar (1893). *Vue sur le ciel : fenêtre de toit de la « Maison Hankar » (1893).* Mit Blick in den Himmel: Das Oberlicht im »Maison Hankar« (1893).
Photo: akg-images / Hilbich

46/47 Welcome: an opulent entrance hall designed by Lionel Jadot. *Bienvenue : entrée superbement dessinée par Lionel Jadot.* Willkommen: Eine von Lionel Jadot prachtvoll gestaltete Lobby.
Photo: Jean-Luc Laloux

48/49 Seen from an unusual angle: view of a dining room furnished by Lionel Jadot. *A travers deux cercles : vue de la salle à manger aménagée par Lionel Jadot.* Eingekreist: Blick ins von Lionel Jadot eingerichtete Esszimmer.
Photo: Jean-Luc Laloux

50/51 Contrasts: rustic furniture and a glamorous chandelier. *Contrastes : mobilier rustique et lustre glamour.* Gegensätze: Ländlich anmutende Möbel und ein glamouröser Leuchter.
Design: Lionel Jadot; Photo: Jean-Luc Laloux

52/53 The heart of the house: cosy drawing room in the style of Lionel Jadot. *Au cœur de la maison : un salon séduisant dans le style de Lionel Jadot.* Das Herz des Hauses: Einladender Salon im Stil von Lionel Jadot.
Photo: Jean-Luc Laloux

54/55 Where Europe meets Asia: living room full of stylistic contrasts. *Quand l'Europe rencontre l'Asie : style mixte pour ce séjour contrasté.* Wo Europa Asien trifft: Wohnzimmer im kontrastreichen Stilmix.
Design: Lionel Jadot; Photo: Jean-Luc Laloux

56/57 Art above the fireplace: the strictly symmetrical style of Lionel Jadot. *Art et cheminée : aspiration à la symétrie, Lionel Jadot oblige.* Kunst am Kamin: Im symmetrie bewussten Look von Lionel Jadot.
Photo: Jean-Luc Laloux

58/59 Well protected: a bedroom under heavy roof beams. *Bien protégée : chambre à coucher avec grosses poutres apparentes.* Gut abgeschirmt: Schlafzimmer unter dicken Dachbalken.
Design: Lionel Jadot; Photo: Jean-Luc Laloux

60/61 Art in the kitchen: another example of interior design by Lionel Jadot. *Art dans une cuisine : autre intérieur dessiné par Lionel Jadot.* Kunst in der Küche: Ebenfalls ein Interieurdesign von Lionel Jadot.
Photo: Jean-Luc Laloux

62/63 Old and new: design inspired by the Ancient World with modern touches. *Ancien et nouveau : accents modernes sur un design antique, dans la salle de bains.* Alt und neu: Antikes Design und moderne Akzente im Bad. *Design: Lionel Jadot; Photo: Jean-Luc Laloux*

64/65 Gazing across the room: portrait of a lady above the fireplace. *Saisir l'éphémère : portrait de femme au-dessus de la cheminée.* Nur ein Augenblick: Frauenporträt über dem Kamin. *Architect: Alex van de Walle; Photo: Jean-Luc Laloux*

66/67 Beneath the ancient beams: a room in pale blue. *Sous d'antiques poutres : chambre au gris-bleu délicat.* Unter antiken Deckenbalken: Zimmer in zartem Graublau. *Architect: Alex van de Walle; Photo: Jean-Luc Laloux*

68/69 Exhibition space: objets d'art on a coffee table. *Plan d'exposition : objets d'art sur la table du séjour.* Ausstellungsfläche: Kunstobjekte auf dem Wohnzimmertisch. *Architect: Alex van de Walle; Photo: Jean-Luc Laloux*

70/71 Contrasts: light and shade on the staircase. *Opposés : contrastes passionnants dans l'escalier.* Gegensätze: Spannende Kontraste im Treppenhaus. *Architect: Alex van de Walle; Photo: Jean-Luc Laloux*

72/73 Touches of beige: a view of the kitchen. *Couleur beige : vue de la cuisine.* In Beige gehalten: Einblick in die Küche. *Architect: Alex van de Walle; Photo: Jean-Luc Laloux*

74/75 Mediterranean style: kitchen with open shelves and wicker baskets. *Dans le style du Sud : cuisine avec casiers de rangement ouverts et vanneries.* Im Stil des Südens: Küche mit offenen Regalen und Korbwaren. *Architect: Alex van de Walle; Photo: Jean-Luc Laloux*

76/77 Soft light streams through large livingroom windows. *Magie des grandes fenêtres : une douce lumière baigne le salon.* Dank großer Fenster: Weiches Licht in einem Wohnraum. *Interior Design: Axel Vervoordt; Photo: Jean-Luc Laloux*

78/79 An almost spiritual feel: room designed by the art dealer Axel Vervoordt. *Atmosphère presque spirituelle : aménagement de l'espace par le collectionneur d'art Axel Vervoordt.* Fast spirituelle Atmosphäre: Raumdesign des Kunstsammlers Axel Vervoordt. *Photo: Jean-Luc Laloux*

80/81 Different woods in harmony: an idea from Axel Vervoordt. *Harmonie des essences : une idée d'Axel Vervoordt.* Verschiedene Hölzer in Harmonie: Eine Idee von Axel Vervoordt. *Photo: Jean-Luc Laloux*

82/83 Warm and cosy: a traditional tiled fireplace. *Source de chaleur : la cheminée et son pourtour de faïences, dans le style traditionnel.* Wärmequelle: Im traditionellen Stil umkachelter Kamin. *Interior Design: Axel Vervoordt; Photo: Jean-Luc Laloux*

84/85 In front of an open fire: comfortable sitting room designed by Axel Vervoordt. *Près de la cheminée ouverte : espace confortable pour s'asseoir, aménagé par Axel Vervoordt.* Am offenen Kamin: Gemütlicher Sitzbereich, gestaltet von Axel Vervoordt. *Photo: Jean-Luc Laloux*

86/87 Polished floors add sparkle to an Axel Vervoordt interior. *Sur du parquet brillant : un intérieur d'Axel Vervoordt.* Auf glänzendem Parkett: Ein Interieur von Axel Vervoordt. *Photo: Jean-Luc Laloux*

88/89 A view of the garden: beautifully simple dining room. *Vue sur la nature : salle à manger sobre et belle.* Mit Blick ins Grüne: Schlichtschönes Esszimmer. *Interior Design: Axel Vervoordt; Photo: Jean-Luc Laloux*

90/91 A splash of colour by the window: a brilliant red chaise longue. *Touche de couleur près de la fenêtre : méridienne d'un rouge lumineux.* Farbtupfer am Fenster: Eine leuchtend rote Chaiselongue. *Interior Design: Axel Vervoordt; Photo: Jean-Luc Laloux*

92/93 Well-lit: a stylish and symmetrical Brussels dining room. *Bien éclairée : salle à manager bruxelloise – style et symétrie.* Gut beleuchtet: Brüsseler Esszimmer mit Stil und Symmetrie. *Photo: Jean-Luc Laloux*

94/95 Window onto the staircase: plenty of open space in a house built by Jos Reynders. *Fenêtre sur escalier : beaucoup d'espace et de largeur dans cette maison construite par Jos Reynders.* Fensterfront zum Treppenhaus: Viel Raum und Weite im von Jos Reynders erbauten Haus.

96/97 Inviting and elegant: tall double doors in a Jos Reynders house. *Charme et élégance : haute porte à deux vantaux dans une maison construite par Jos Reynders.* Einladend und elegant: Hohe Flügeltüren in einem von Jos Reynders erbauten Haus. *Photo: Jean-Luc Laloux*

98/99 Everything in its place: a well-organised study. *A quatre épingles : bureau bien ordonné.* In Reih und Glied: Ordentlich aufgeräumtes Arbeitszimmer. *Photo: Jean-Luc Laloux*

100/101 Kitchen quartet: four chairs in a Jos Reynders house. *Mobilier en quatuor : quatre chaises de cuisine dans une maison construite par Jos Reynders.* Möbel im Quartett: Vier Küchenstühle in einem von Jos Reynders erbauten Haus. *Photo: Jean-Luc Laloux*

102/103 Like sleeping in the clouds: a four-poster bed in a bright bedroom. *Dormir au septième ciel : lit à baldaquin dans une chambre à coucher lumineuse.* Schlafen wie auf Wolken: Himmelbett im hellen Schlafzimmer. *Photo: Jean-Luc Laloux*

104/105 Elegant curves: washstand and bath tub. *Belles courbes : lavabo et baignoire élégantes.* Schön geschwungen: Eleganter Waschtisch und Badewanne. *Photo: Jean-Luc Laloux*

106/107 Rhapsody in blue: Agnes Emery's kitchen. *Heure bleue : dans la cuisine d'Agnès Emery.* Blaue Stunde: In der Küche von Agnes Emery. *Photo: Alexander van Berge / Taverne Agency*

108/109 Mirror, mirror on the wall: the home of designer Agnes Emery. *Miroir, mon beau miroir : chez la dessinatrice Agnès Emery.* Spieglein, Spieglein an der Wand: Bei der Designerin Agnes Emery. *Photo: Alexander van Berge / Taverne Agency*

110/111 Rounded arches and a long table chez Agnes Emery. *Sous des arcs plein cintre : longue table chez Agnès Emery.* Raum unter Rundbögen: Lange Tafel bei Agnes Emery. *Photo: Alexander van Berge / Taverne Agency*

112/113 A sense of order: shelves lining the walls in Eugénie Collet's dining room. *Le sens de l'ordre : que des étagères dans la salle à manger d'Eugénie Collet.* Mit Sinn für Ordnung: Regalwände im Esszimmer von Eugénie Collet. *Photo: S. Anton / Inside*

114/115 Everything's all white: the home of set designer Eugénie Collet. *Tout en blanc : dans la maison de la chef décoratrice Eugénie Collet.* Ganz in Weiß: Im Haus der Set-Designerin Eugénie Collet. *Photo: S. Anton / Inside*

116/117 A doctor's waiting room, maybe? Another view of Eugénie Collet's house. *En attendant le médecin ? Egalement chez Eugénie Collet.* Warten, bis der Arzt kommt? Ebenfalls bei Eugénie Collet. *Photo: S. Anton / Inside*

118/119 Sleeping with simplicity: the home of set designer Eugénie Collet. *Dormir sobrement : dans la maison de la chef décoratrice Eugénie Collet.* Schlicht schlafen: Im Haus der Set-Designerin Eugénie Collet. *Photo: S. Anton / Inside*

120/121 A place by the window: in Eugénie Collet's brightly lit work room. *Une place à la fenêtre : dans le lumineux bureau d'Eugénie Collet.* Ein Fensterplatz: Im hellen Arbeitszimmer von Eugénie Collet. *Photo: S. Anton / Inside*

122/123 Art from floor to ceiling: a dining room with a studio atmosphere. *De l'art, du sol au plafond : salle à manger avec atmosphère d'atelier.* Kunst vom Boden bis zur Decke: Im Esszimmer mit Atelier-Atmosphäre. *Architects: Bataille-Ibens; Photo: Jean-Luc Laloux*

124/125 Sitting around: a pale sofa and darker armchair. *En rond : sofa clair et fauteuils foncés.* Eine runde Sache: Helles Sofa und dunklere Sessel. *Architects: Bataille-Ibens; Photo: Jean-Luc Laloux*

126/127 Partition walls reminiscent of a stage set: a living room designed by Bataille-Ibens. *Des cloisons comme au théâtre : un séjour des architectes Bataille-Ibens.* Trennwände, fast wie im Theater: Ein Wohnzimmer der Architekten Bataille-Ibens. *Photo: Jean-Luc Laloux*

128/129 Striking effects: a Bataille-Ibens design. *Plein d'effet : dessiné par Bataille-Ibens.* Effektvolle Elemente: Ein Entwurf von Bataille-Ibens. *Photo: Jean-Luc Laloux*

130/131 Neatly arranged: works of the private art collection. *Distribuées : œuvres d'art, composition du propriétaire.* Aufgefächert: Kunstwerke, aus der Privatsammlung des Besitzers. *Photo: Jean-Luc Laloux*

132/133 Behind dark double doors: a studio designed by Bataille-Ibens. *Derrière de sombres portes à vantaux : bureau, aménagé par Bataille-Ibens.* Hinter dunklen Flügeltüren: Arbeitszimmer, gestaltet von Bataille-Ibens. *Photo: Jean-Luc Laloux*

134/135 And so to bed: room for an art lover in a Bataille-Ibens house. *Bien bordé : chambre à coucher artistique dans une maison des architectes Bataille-Ibens.* Gut gebettet: Im kunstsinnigen Schlafzimmer eines Hauses der Architekten Bataille-Ibens. *Photo: Jean-Luc Laloux*

136/137 Beautifully simple: living and dining area designed by Vincent van Duysen. *Sobre et beau : espace salon et salle à manger, dessiné par Vincent van Duysen.* Schön schlicht: Wohn- und Essbereich im Design von Vincent van Duysen. *Photo: Jean-Luc Laloux*

138/139 Spacious: two views of a living room designed by Vincent van Duysen. *Grandes surfaces : deux tableaux dans un séjour de Vincent van Duysen.* Großflächig: Zwei Bilder in einem Wohnzimmer von Vincent van Duysen gestaltet. *Photo: Jean-Luc Laloux*

140/141 Transparency and tone-on-tone colour: Vincent van Duysen's characteristic style. *Transparence ton sur ton : le style de Vincent van Duysen.* Transparenz, Ton in Ton: Der Stil von Vincent van Duysen. *Photo: Jean-Luc Laloux*

142/143 Working environment: a living space minimally furnished by Vincent van Duysen. *Atmosphère de travail : aménagement minimaliste dans cette pièce réalisée par van Duysen.* Arbeitsatmosphäre: Ein von van Duysen minimalistisch ausgestatteter Raum. *Photo: Jean-Luc Laloux*

144/145 Seen from a different angle: view of the kitchen. *Penser en coin : aperçu de la cuisine.* Um die Ecke gedacht: Blick in die Küche. *Photo: Jean-Luc Laloux*

146/147 Light reflected on the wall of a van Duysen kitchen. *Reflets de lumière : au mur d'une cuisine van Duysen.* Lichtreflexe: An der Wand einer van-Duysen-Küche. *Photo: Jean-Luc Laloux*

148/149 Cuboid kitchen: a minimalist design by Vincent van Duysen. *Cuisine rectangle : conception minimaliste de Vincent van Duysen.* Küchenquader: Ein minimalistischer Entwurf von Vincent van Duysen. *Photo: Jean-Luc Laloux*

150/151 White wall cupboards provide storage space for toiletries. *Derrière des placards blancs : espace de rangement pour les accessoires de bain.* Hinter weißen Wandschränken: Stauraum für Bad-Accessoires. *Design: Vincent van Duysen; Photo: Jean-Luc Laloux*

152/153 View from the bed: a Vincent van Duysen bedroom. *Vue depuis le lit : dans une chambre à coucher de Vincent van Duysen.* Ausblick vom Bett aus: In einem Schlafzimmer von Vincent van Duysen. *Photo: Jean-Luc Laloux*

154/155 Sideboard with a splash of colour: a design by Vincent van Duysen. *Sideboard avec touche de couleur : le design est de Vincent van Duysen.* Sideboard mit Farbtupfer: Ein Entwurf von Vincent van Duysen. *Photo: Jean-Luc Laloux*

" ... such a great looking-glass stood on my dressing-table – such a fine mirror glittered over the mantelpiece ... "

Charlotte Brontë, in: _The Professor_

« ... Un verre aussi magnifique était posé sur ma coiffeuse – un miroir aussi beau brillait au-dessus de la cheminée ... »

Charlotte Brontë, dans : _Le Professeur_

» ... Solch großartiges Glas stand auf meiner Frisierkommode – solch ein schöner Spiegel glitzerte über dem Kamin ... «

Charlotte Brontë, in: _Der Professor_

DETAILS

Détails   Details

165 An entrance hall by Lionel Jadot. *Accueil dans une entrée de Lionel Jadot.* Empfang in einer Lobby von Lionel Jadot. *Photo: Jean-Luc Laloux*

166 An interesting twist: view of a staircase. *Bon pied, bon œil : un escalier fascinant.* Den Dreh raushaben: Faszinierendes Treppenhaus. *Architect: Alex van de Walle; Photo: Jean-Luc Laloux*

167 At the foot of the stairs: a small statue. *Au pied de l'escalier : petite sculpture.* Am Fuß der Treppe: eine kleine Skulptur. *Architect: Alex van de Walle; Photo: Jean-Luc Laloux*

169 Echoes of the ancient world: raised bath designed by Lionel Jadot. *Patinée : baignoire surélevée, dessinée par Lionel Jadot.* Mit Patina: Erhöhte Wanne im Design von Lionel Jadot. *Photo: Jean-Luc Laloux*

170 Comfort zone: pillows with filigree pattern. *Douillets : oreillers avec motifs en filigrane.* Weich gebettet: Kissen mit filigranen Mustern. *Photo: Alexander van Berge / Taverne Agency*

171 Starstruck: tiles in the home of Agnes Emery. *Décrochées du ciel : des étoiles sur les faïences d'Agnès Emery.* Vom Himmel geholt: Sterne auf Fliesen bei Agnes Emery. *Photo: Alexander van Berge / Taverne Agency*

173 Sweet dreams guaranteed: Agnes Emery's bed. *Beaux rêves garantis : le lit d'Agnès Emery.* Süße Träume garantiert. Das Bett von Agnes Emery. *Photo: Alexander van Berge / Taverne Agency*

174 Smells good! Agnes Emery's cat investigates. *Quel parfum ! Le chat d'Agnès Emery.* Wie das duftet! Die Katze von Agnes Emery. *Photo: Alexander van Berge / Taverne Agency*

175 Mirrors on the wall chez Agnes Emery. *Mur de miroirs chez Agnès Emery.* Spiegelwand bei Agnes Emery. *Photo: Alexander van Berge / Taverne Agency*

176 Freshly prepared: salad à la Agnes Emery. *Tout juste préparée : salade à la Agnès Emery.* Frisch zubereitet: Salat à la Agnes Emery. *Photo: Alexander van Berge / Taverne Agency*

178 Multi-level: staircase in Agnes Emery's house. *Etagé : l'escalier chez Agnès Emery.* Abgestuft: Treppenhaus bei Agnes Emery. *Photo: Alexander van Berge / Taverne Agency*

179 Full of vitamins: Agnes Emery's kitchen. *Plein de vitamines : la cuisine d'Agnès Emery.* Voller Vitamine: Agnes Emerys Küche. *Photo: Alexander van Berge / Taverne Agency*

181 The colourful world of books: a bookshelf in Agnes Emery's house. *Le monde bariolé des livres : une étagère chez Agnès Emery.* Die bunte Welt der Bücher: Regal bei Agnes Emery. *Photo: Alexander van Berge / Taverne Agency*

182 Framed in white: doors in Agnes Emery's house. *Aux cadres blancs : portes chez Agnès Emery. Weiße Rahmen: Türen im Haus von Agnes Emery. Photo: Alexander van Berge / Taverne Agency*

183 Inspired by the Orient: cushions in Agnes Emery's house. *D'inspiration orientale : coussins chez Agnès Emery. Orientalisch inspiriert: Kissen bei Agnes Emery. Photo: Alexander van Berge / Taverne Agency*

185 Pink Paradise: Agnes Emery's magical sofa. *Paradis en rose : sofa ravissant chez Agnès Emery. Paradies in Pink: Zauberhaftes Sofa bei Agnes Emery. Photo: Alexander van Berge / Taverne Agency*

186 Stacked up: clay bowls chez Agnes Emery. *Empilés : bols en terre chez Agnès Emery. Stapelweise: Tonschalen bei Agnes Emery. Photo: Alexander van Berge / Taverne Agency*

187 Branching out: chair beside a pile of wood in Agnes Emery's house. *Ramifications : chaise et bûches empilées chez Agnès Emery. Verästelt: Stuhl und Holzscheite bei Agnes Emery. Photo: Alexander van Berge / Taverne Agency*

189 A house in harmony with nature: dining area in the style of van Duysen. *Maison en harmonie avec la nature : espace repas dans le style de van Duysen. Natur und Haus in Harmonie: Essplatz im Stil von van Duysen. Photo: Jean-Luc Laloux*

TASCHEN's London
Ed. Angelika Taschen
Hardcover, 400 pp. / € 29.99 /
$ 39.99 / £ 27.99 / ¥ 5.900

TASCHEN's New York
Ed. Angelika Taschen
Hardcover, 400 pp. / € 29.99 /
$ 39.99 / £ 27.99 / ¥ 5.900

TASCHEN's Paris
Ed. Angelika Taschen
Hardcover, 400 pp. / € 29.99 /
$ 39.99 / £ 27.99 / ¥ 5.900

"This is one for the coffee table, providing more than enough material for a good drool. Gorgeousness between the cover." —*Time Out*, London, on *Great Escapes Africa*

" Buy them all and add some pleasure to your life."

60s Fashion
Ed. Jim Heimann

African Style
Ed. Angelika Taschen

Woody Allen
Ed. Paul Duncan, Glenn Hopp

Architecture Now!
Ed. Philip Jodidio

Art Now
Eds. Burkhard Riemschneider,
Uta Grosenick

Bahia Style
Ed. Angelika Taschen

Bamboo Style
Ed. Angelika Taschen

**Barcelona,
Restaurants & More**
Ed. Angelika Taschen

**Barcelona,
Shops & More**
Ed. Angelika Taschen

Ingrid Bergman
Ed. Paul Duncan, Scott Eyman

Berlin Style
Ed. Angelika Taschen

Humphrey Bogart
Ed. Paul Duncan, James Ursini

Marlon Brando
Ed. Paul Duncan, F.X. Feeney

Brussels Style
Ed. Angelika Taschen

Charlie Chaplin
Ed. Paul Duncan, David Robinson

China Style
Ed. Angelika Taschen

James Dean
Ed. Paul Duncan, F.X. Feeney

Robert De Niro
Ed. Paul Duncan, James Ursini

Johnny Depp
Ed. Paul Duncan, F.X. Feeney

Design Handbook
Charlotte & Peter Fiell

Design for the 21ˢᵗ Century
Eds. Charlotte & Peter Fiell

Marlene Dietrich
Ed. Paul Duncan, James Ursini

Robert Doisneau
Jean-Claude Gautrand

Bob Dylan
Luke Crampton, Dafydd Rees

Clint Eastwood
Ed. Paul Duncan, Douglas
Keesey

Egypt Style
Ed. Angelika Taschen

M.C. Escher

Fashion
Ed. The Kyoto Costume Institute

Fashion Now!
Eds. Terry Jones, Susie
Rushton

Fruit
Ed. George Brookshaw,
Uta Pellgrü-Gagel

Greta Garbo
Ed. Paul Duncan, David
Robinson

HR Giger
HR Giger

Cary Grant
Ed. Paul Duncan, F.X. Feeney

Graphic Design
Eds. Charlotte & Peter Fiell

Greece Style
Ed. Angelika Taschen

Halloween
Ed. Jim Heimann, Steven Heller

Havana Style
Ed. Angelika Taschen

Audrey Hepburn
Ed. Paul Duncan, F.X. Feeney

Katharine Hepburn
Ed. Paul Duncan, Alain Silver

Grace Kelly
Ed. Paul Duncan, Glenn Hopp

London, Restaurants & More
Ed. Angelika Taschen

London, Shops & More
Ed. Angelika Taschen

Bob Marley
Luke Crampton, Dafydd Rees

Marx Brothers
Ed. Paul Duncan, Douglas
Keesey

Steve McQueen
Ed. Paul Duncan, Alain Silver

Miami Style
Ed. Angelika Taschen

Minimal Style
Ed. Angelika Taschen

Marilyn Monroe
Ed. Paul Duncan, F.X. Feeney

Morocco Style
Ed. Angelika Taschen

Paris Style
Ed. Angelika Taschen

Safari Style
Ed. Angelika Taschen

Seaside Style Vol. 2
Ed. Angelika Taschen

Signs
Ed. Julius Wiedeman

South African Style
Ed. Angelika Taschen

Starck
Philippe Starck

Sweden Style
Ed. Angelika Taschen

Tattoos
Ed. Henk Schiffmacher

Tokyo Style
Ed. Angelika Taschen

Valentines
Ed. Jim Heimann, Steven Heller

Web Design: Best Studios
Ed. Julius Wiedemann

Web Design: Best Studios 2
Ed. Julius Wiedemann

Web Design: E-Commerce
Ed. Julius Wiedemann

Web Design: Flash Sites
Ed. Julius Wiedemann

**Web Design: Interactive &
Games**
Ed. Julius Wiedemann

Web Design: Music Sites
Ed. Julius Wiedemann

Web Design: Video Sites
Ed. Julius Wiedemann

Web Design: Portfolios
Ed. Julius Wiedemann

Orson Welles
Ed. Paul Duncan, F.X. Feeney

ICONS